Winner

Student Book 1

Eduardo Amos
Elisabeth Prescher
John Raby

LONGMAN

Contents......

Get ready!

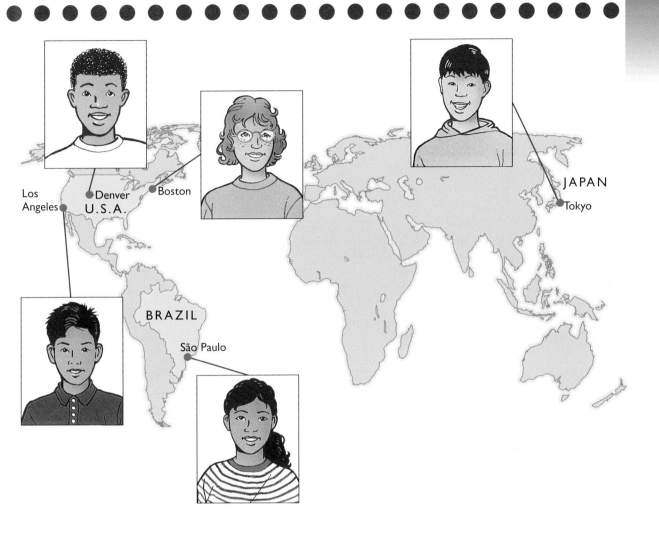

Los
Angeles

Denver
U.S.A.

Boston

BRAZIL

São Paulo

JAPAN

Tokyo

*We're on
vacation
in
Florida!*

PM
27 AUG
1998

William T Pip...
Aviation Pioneer
40

UNIT 1

Hi!

1. 🔲 **Listen and practice.**

A.

MARIANA: Hi!

HIROSHI: Hi!

MARIANA: My name's Mariana. What's your name?

HIROSHI: My name's Hiroshi.

B.

MARIANA: Hi, Bill!

BILL: Hi, Mariana!

HIROSHI: Hi! My name's Hiroshi.
What's your name?

BILL: Hello, Hiroshi. My name's Bill.

 SPEAKING

2. **Read and practice.**

| What's your name?
My name's Hiroshi. | _____
_____ |

3. **Talk to a friend.**

Example:

A: Hi!

B: Hello!

A: What's your name?

B: My name's _____. What's your name?

A: My name's _____.

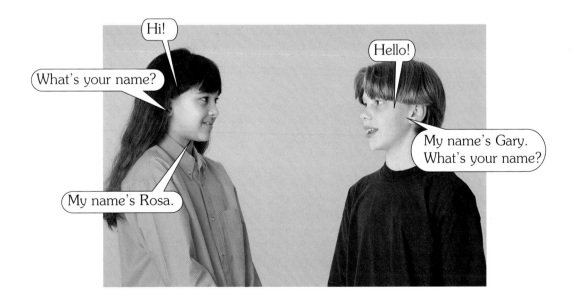

LISTENING

4. 📼 Listen and check the correct picture.

1.
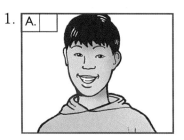  

2.
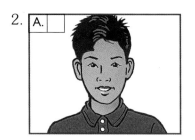  

3.

4.

5. 📼 Listen and practice.

 WRITING

6. **Write the names like this.**

My name's *CATHY*.

1.

My name's _ _ _ _ _ _ _ _ _.

2.

My name's _ _ _ _ .

My name's _ _ _ _ .

My name's _ _ _ _ _ _ _ _ .

3.

4.

5.

7. **Fill in the card on the right with your names.**

Mariana   Lemos
first name   family name

_____   _____
first name   family name

 SPEAKING

8. **Ask each other about your names.**

What's your | first / family | name?

My | first / family | name's _____ .

READING

9. Read the cards. Then fill in the blanks in the chart below.

1.

SOCCER CLUB

first name Mike
family name Jones

2.
SOCCER CLUB

first name Claudia
family name Ramos

3.

SOCCER CLUB

first name John
family name Wong

	first name	family name
1.		*Jones*
2.	*Claudia*	
3.		

10. Write dialogs between you and a friend. Follow the example for your *first* and *family* names.

A: Hi!

B: _Hi!_ What's _your first name_?

A: My first name's _____. What's _____ _____ _____?

B: My first name's _____.

Look what you know!

GRAMMAR

VERB to be
is   My name's Juan. (My name is Juan.)

POSSESSIVE ADJECTIVES
my   My name's Juan.
your   What's your name?

QUESTION
What's your name? (What is your name?)

ANSWER
My name's Bill.

WORD BANK

Hi!   name
Hello!   first
           family

LEARN SOME
WORDS

1. Translate these words. Then find them in the picture below.

a T-shirt   sneakers   shorts   a sweat shirt   a tennis shirt   socks   a shirt

READ SOME
MORE

2. Read and match.

> 1. Hello! My name's Chan-Woo Park.
>   I'm from Seoul.

> 2. Hello! My name's Margarita
>   Martinez. I'm from Mexico City.

> 3. Hi! My name's Caroline Lin.
>   I'm from Taipei.

> 4. Hi! My name's Tono Diaz.
>   I'm from Lima.

A. *3*   B.   C.   D.

3. Write what they are wearing.

Margarita is wearing a T-shirt.

LISTEN
IN

4. 🖭 Listen and fill in the chart.

	first name	family name	town
1.	*Catalina*		
2.		*Nikolaon*	

NOW YOU'RE
TALKING!

5. Talk to another student. Talk to your teacher.

What's your first name?
What's your family name?
How do you spell that?
Where are you from?

UNIT 2

Her name's Sandra.

1. 📼 **Listen and practice.**

A.

MARIANA: Hi, Juan!

JUAN: Hello, Mariana!

MARIANA: Juan, this is my father. His name's Mario Lemos.

JUAN: Hello, Mr. Lemos. Nice to meet you.

MR. LEMOS: Nice to meet you, Juan.

B.

MARIANA: This is my sister.
Her name's Sandra.

JUAN: Nice to meet you, Sandra.

C.

MARIANA: This is my brother.
His name's Paulo.

JUAN: Nice to meet you, Paulo.

 SPEAKING

2. Read and practice.

This is my friend.
Her name's Cathy.

Nice to meet you, Cathy.

A: This is my friend.

His/Her name's _____.

B: Nice to meet you, _____.

 SPEAKING

3. Look at the pictures and ask about their names.

What's his name?	_____
What's her name?	_____

1. A: What's his name?

   B: His name's Tom Hanks.

2. A: What's her name?

   B: Her name's Whoopi Goldberg.

3. A: What's _____ name?

   B: _____ _____ Gloria Estefan.

4. A: What's _____ name?

   B: _____ _____ Keanu Reeves.

5. A: What's _____ _____?

   B: _____ _____ Sandra Bullock.

6. A: What's _____ _____?

   B: _____ _____ Brad Pitt.

4. **This is Mariana's family. Take turns introducing Mariana's family.**

This is her sister. This is her brother.	_____ _____

1. Alice Lemos
(mother)

2. Mario Lemos
(father)

3. Paulo Lemos
(brother)

Mariana Lemos

4. Sandra Lemos
(sister)

1. This is her mother. Her name's Alice.

2. This is her father. His name's Mario.

3. This is her _____. _____ name's Paulo.

4. This is her _____. _____ name's Sandra.

 LISTENING

5. 🎞 **Listen and number the pictures.**

A. ☐

B. ☐

C. *1*

D. ☐

READING

البحث

READING

6. **Read about Cathy's family.**

> My name is Cathy. This is my family: my father, my mother, my brother, my sister, and me.
>
> This is my father. His name's David. His nickname's Dave. This is my mother. Her name's Jane. Her nickname's Janey. This is my brother. His name's Philip. His nickname's Phil. This is my sister. Her name's Janet. Her nickname's Jan.

7. **Fill in the chart about Cathy's family.**

	father	mother	brother	sister
name	David			
nickname	Dave			

○ ○

 WRITING

8. Look at Cathy's family. Fill in the blanks and answer the questions.

1. This is her _sister_. What's her name?
   Her name's Janet.
   Her nickname's Jan.

2. This is her _____. What's her name?
   _____
   _____

3. This is her _____. What's his name?
   _____
   _____

4. This is her _____. What's his name?
   _____
   _____

Look what you know!

GRAMMAR

POSSESSIVE ADJECTIVES
his   His name's Diego.
her   Her name's Sandra.

DEMONSTRATIVE PRONOUN
this   This is my brother.

WORD BANK

father   nickname
mother
brother
sister
friend

EXTRA!

LEARN SOME WORDS

1. Translate these words. Then write them in the picture below.

door   window   clock   blackboard   desk   chair   student   teacher

READ SOME MORE

2. Read about Alex's class. Write the numbers with the names.

A. *clock*

B.

C.

D.

E.

F.

G.

H.

My name is Alex Nikolaon [*1*]. This is my teacher, two other students from my class, and me. My teacher is from Los Angeles. Her name is Mrs. Jennifer Baker [   ]. This is Jin-ha Kim [   ]. He's from Seoul. This is Zeynep Aslan [   ]. She's from Ankara.

LISTEN IN

3. 🎦 **Listen and match the names with the people.**

1. Joey
2. Elizabeth
3. Sandy
4. Frederick
5. John

4. 🎦 **Listen and draw a picture.**

NOW YOU'RE TALKING!

5. Talk to another student. Talk to your teacher.

　 What's your nickname?
　 Who's this?
　 What's his name?
　 What's her name?

REVIEW
UNITS 1-2

I. **Complete the conversations.**

1. JUAN: Hi! My name's Juan.
    What's *your* ___name___?
    MARIANA: My name's *Mariana* .

2. JUAN: What's her name?
    BILL: _____ _____ Mariana.

3. CATHY: What's _____ _____ ?
    HIROSHI: His name's Bill.

4. MARIANA: This is _____ sister.
    Her name's Sandra.
    CATHY: _____ _____ _____ you,
    Sandra.

2. **Write the questions.**

1. *What's his name?* _____ His name's Paul.
2. _____ Her name's Lucy.
3. _____ My name's Karen.
4. _____ Her name's Cathy.
5. _____ My name's John.
6. _____ His name's Bob.

3. **Look at Mary's family. Then fill in the blanks in the chart.**

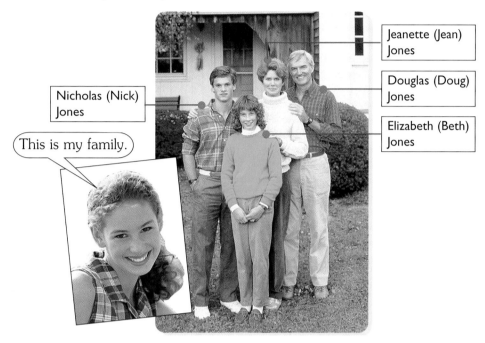

	mother	father	sister	brother
first	*Jeanette*			
nickname				*Nick*

4. **Write about Mary's family.**

1. Jeanette is *her   mother* .

   What's *her* nickname?

   Her nickname's *Jean* .

2. Douglas is _____ _____ .

   What's _____ nickname?

   His nickname's _____ .

3. Elizabeth is _____ _____ .

   What's _____ nickname?

   _____ _____ _____ .

4. Nicholas is _____ _____ .

   What's _____ nickname?

   _____ _____ _____ .

Now you're ready for the test!

UNIT 3

Is he Cathy's friend?

1.  **Listen and practice.**

A.

HIROSHI: Good morning, Cathy!

CATHY: Good morning, Hiroshi. This is my friend, Alan.

HIROSHI: Hi, Alan!

ALAN: Hi, Hiroshi. Nice to meet you.

CATHY: Well, goodbye, Hiroshi.

ALAN: Bye.

HIROSHI: Goodbye.

B.

JUAN: Is he Cathy's brother?

HIROSHI: No, he isn't.

JUAN: Is he Cathy's friend?

HIROSHI: Yes, he is.

SPEAKING

2. Listen and practice.

1. Good morning.

2. Good afternoon.

3. Good evening.

4. Goodbye. Bye.

3. Practice the greetings.

 SPEAKING

4. **Talk about Cathy's family.**

| She's Cathy's mother.
He's Cathy's father. | _____
_____ |

1.

Jane Hart
(mother)

+

2.

David Hart
(father)

3.

Phil
(brother)

4.

Janet
(sister)

Cathy

1. She's Cathy's mother.

2. _____ Cathy's father.

3. _____ Cathy's brother.

4. _____ Cathy's sister.

5. **Talk about Cathy's family and friends. Practice the dialogs.**

| Yes, she is.
No, she isn't. | _____
_____ |

Phil

Jane

1. father/brother
   A: Is he Cathy's father?
   B: No, he isn't.
   A: Is he Cathy's brother?
   B: Yes, he is.

2. sister/mother
   A: Is she Cathy's sister?
   B: No, she isn't.
   A: Is she Cathy's mother?
   B: Yes, she is.

David

Mariana

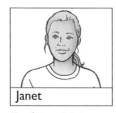
Janet

Alan

3. brother/father   4. sister/friend   5. friend/sister   6. brother/friend

 LISTENING

6. Listen and check the correct picture.

1.
A.
B. ✓
C.

2.
A.
B.
C.

3.
A.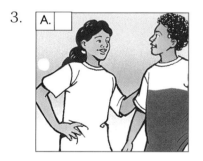
B.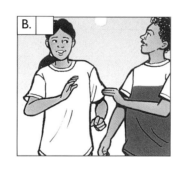
C.

4.
A.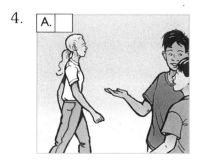
B.
C.

5.
A.
B.
C.

READING

7. **Read and circle the correct answer. Fill in the boxes with their names.**

This is Homer. He's my father. This is Marge. She's my mother. This is Bart. He isn't my friend. He's my brother. This is Maggie. She's my sister. What's my name?

My name is   a. Bart
              b. Lisa
              c. Marge

 WRITING

8. **Write about Lisa's family.**

Homer

1. Homer isn't her brother. *He's her father.*

2. Marge isn't her sister. _____

3. Maggie isn't her mother. _____

4. Bart isn't her father. _____

9. **Answer the questions about Lisa's family.**

1. Is Marge her mother? *Yes, she is.*

2. Is Homer her brother? *No, he isn't.*

3. Is Maggie her sister? _____

4. Is Bart her father? _____

5. Is Homer her father? _____

6. Is Marge her sister? _____

Look what you know!

GRAMMAR

VERB to be

QUESTION
Is he Cathy's brother?

ANSWERS
Yes, he is.
No, he isn't.

PERSONAL PRONOUNS
he   He's Cathy's father.
she   She's Cathy's mother.

WORD BANK

Good morning
Good afternoon
Good evening
Goodbye
Bye

LEARN SOME WORDS ▸ **1.** **Translate these words. Then find them in the picture below.**

yard   living room   kitchen   bathroom   bedroom   dining room   garage   house

READ SOME MORE ▸ **2.** **Read about Mary's family.**

1. Hi! My name is Mary Jones. This is my house. This is my family: my father, my mother, my brother, my sister, my friend, and me.

2. Is this her mother? No, it isn't. It's her sister, Elizabeth Jones.

3. Is this her mother? Yes, it is. It's her mother, Jeanette Jones.

4. Is this her sister? No, it isn't. It's her friend, Mariana.

5. Is this her brother? Yes, it is. It's her brother, Nicholas Jones.

6. Is this Mary's father? Yes it is. It's her father, Douglas Jones.

3. **Point to the people and ask questions.**

LISTEN
IN

4. 📼 **Listen and number the pictures.**

A. ☐   Peru

B. ☐   South Korea

C. ☐   Mexico

D. ☐   Taiwan

5. Write the dialogs for the other two pictures.

NOW YOU'RE
TALKING!

6. Draw a picture of your family and friends. Talk to another student. Talk to your teacher. Talk about your friends and your family.

▪ Is he your friend?
▪ Is she your friend?
▪ Is she your mother?
▪ Is he your father?
▪ Is he your brother?
▪ Is she your sister?

How are you?

1. 🔊 **Listen and practice.**

A.

JUAN: Hi, Bill.
BILL: Hi, Juan. How are you?
JUAN: I'm fine, thanks. How are you?
BILL: I'm . . . uh . . .
JUAN: Are you tired?
BILL: No, I'm not tired. I'm sad.

B.

CATHY: Is Bill tired?
JUAN: No, he isn't. He's sad.
CATHY: What's the matter?
JUAN: His girlfriend. Look.

girlfriend	_____
boyfriend	_____

 SPEAKING

2. 🔊 **Listen and practice.**

1. She's fine.

2. He's tired.

3. She's happy.

4. He's sad.

5. She's hungry.

6. He's thirsty.

SPEAKING

3. **Read and practice.**

How are you?	_____
I'm sad.	_____
We're happy.	_____

4. **Practice the dialogs.**

1.

2.

3.

4.

5.

6.

5. Read and practice.

| I'm not sad.
We aren't sad. | _____
_____ |

1.

I'm not sad.

2.

We aren't sad.

3.

He isn't happy.

4.

She isn't happy.

WRITING

6. Fill in the blanks.

tired   happy   sad   hungry   thirsty

1. Are you _sad_____? No, I'm _not_____. I'm _happy___.

2. Is he thirsty? No, he _____. He's _____.

3. Is she _____? No, she _____. She's _____.

4. Are you _____? No, we _____. We're _____.

○ ○

 LISTENING

7. 📼 **Listen and number the pictures.**

A.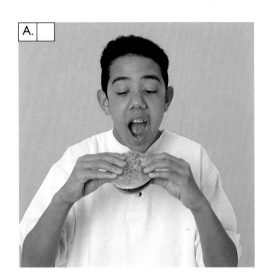

B.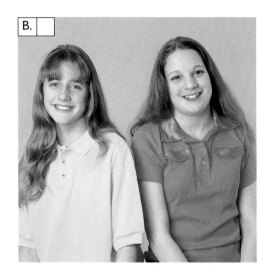

C.

D. *1*

8. 📼 **Listen and check the correct answer.**

	happy	tired	sad	hungry	thirsty
Mariana					
Cathy					
Juan	✓				
Hiroshi					
Bill					

 **READING**

9. Read and identify the people. Write their names in the boxes.

My friends and I are in a restaurant. My name's Jim. I'm hungry. My friend Tom isn't hungry. He's thirsty. His sister Mary isn't thirsty. She's tired. Sally isn't tired. She's sad. Linda isn't sad. She's happy! Today is her birthday!

Jim

10. True or False?

1. Mary is tired. _True_

2. Tom is hungry. _____

3. Jim is thirsty. _____

4. Linda is happy. _____

5. Sally is sad. _____

Look what you know!

11. Write four sentences about you and three friends. Use *tired, sad, happy, fine, hungry,* or *thirsty.*

I'm happy. My friend . . .

GRAMMAR

VERB to be

QUESTION	ANSWERS
Are you happy?	Yes, I am.
	No, I'm not. (I am not)
	Yes, we are.
	No, we aren't. (we are not)

PERSONAL PRONOUN

we   We are happy.

QUESTION	ANSWER
How are you?	I'm fine.

WORD BANK

fine
tired
happy
sad
hungry
thirsty
girlfriend

LEARN SOME WORDS ►

1. **Translate these words. Then find them in the picture below.**

pizza   orange juice   hamburger   salad   french fries   fried chicken
soda   apple pie   ice cream

READ SOME MORE ►

2. **Match these food trays to the correct food order.**

HAMBURGER ～$2
PIZZA ～$2
FRIED CHICKEN $2
FRENCH FRIES $1
SALAD ～～$1

ICE CREAM ～$1
APPLE PIE ～$1
SODA ～～50¢
ORANGE JUICE ～50¢

1. *Juan*

2. _____

3. _____

4. _____

JUAN: A pizza, french fries, ice cream, and a soda, please.

BILL: Fried chicken, a salad, apple pie, and an orange juice, please.

MARIANA: Fried chicken, french fries, ice cream, and a soda, please.

LINDA: A hamburger, french fries, apple pie, and an orange juice, please.

HIROSHI: A pizza, french fries, apple pie, and a soda, please.

CATHY: A hamburger, french fries, ice cream, and an orange juice, please.

3. **Draw the other two food trays.**

4. **Order your own food.**

LISTEN
IN

5. 🖭 **Listen and number the pictures.**

6. Write the dialogs for the other two pictures.

NOW YOU'RE
TALKING!

7. Talk to another student. Talk to your teacher.

 How are you?

 Are you happy?

 Are you sad?

 What's the matter?

 Are you thirsty?

 Are you hungry?

 Are you tired?

 Is today your birthday?

1. Fill in the blanks with *I, you, he,* or *she.*

1. *She* is my mother.
2. _____ are my friend.
3. _____ is my father.
4. _____ am sad.
5. _____ is my sister.
6. _____ am happy.
7. _____ is my brother.
8. _____ are tired.

2. Fill in the blanks with *he, she, his,* or *her.*

1. *His* name is David. *He* is my friend.
2. _____ name is Karen. _____ is my friend.
3. _____ name is Kelly. _____ is my sister.
4. _____ is my brother. _____ name is Dan.
5. _____ name is Edward. _____ is my father.
6. _____ is my mother. _____ name is Sandra.

3. Look at the pictures and answer the questions.

1. Is he Hiroshi?
   Yes, he is.

2. Is she Cathy?
   No, she isn't.

3. Is he Mr. Lemos?
   _____

4. Is he Bill?

_____

5. Is she Mariana?

_____

6. Is he Juan?

_____

4. Look at the pictures and fill in the blanks.

1.

_We_ _aren't_ happy.
We're sad.

2.

_____ _____ hungry.
I'm thirsty.

3.

_____ _____ sad.
She's happy.

4.

_____ _____ thirsty.
He's hungry.

5.

_____ _____ sad.
I'm happy.

6.

_____ _____ sad.
We're tired.

5. Match the columns.

1. Juan isn't tired.   a. We're happy.

2. We aren't sad.   b. I'm thirsty.

3. I'm not hungry.   c. You're hungry.

4. Bob isn't sad.   d. He's sad.

5. You aren't thirsty.   e. He's tired.

Now you're ready for the test!

UNIT 5

How old are you?

1. 📼 **Listen and practice.**

A.

MARIANA: Happy birthday, Cathy!
CATHY: Thank you.
MARIANA: How old are you?
CATHY: I'm twelve. How old are you?
MARIANA: I'm twelve, too.

B.

CATHY: How old are you, Juan?
JUAN: I'm eleven.
CATHY: How old are you, Bill?
BILL: I'm thirteen.

 SPEAKING

2. 📼 **Listen and practice.**

1	2	3	4	5	6	7
one	two	three	four	five	six	seven

8	9	10	11	12	13	14
eight	nine	ten	eleven	twelve	thirteen	fourteen

15	16	17	18	19	20
fifteen	sixteen	seventeen	eighteen	nineteen	twenty

3. Practice the dialog.

| How old are you? | _____ |

A: How old are you?

B: I'm _____ .

4. Read and practice.

| They're seven. | _____ |

1. He's ten.

2. She's fourteen.

3. They're seven.

I'm three.

4. I'm three.

You're twenty.

5. You're twenty.

We're six.

6. We're six.

● ●

SPEAKING

5. **Look at the pictures and practice the dialogs.**

1. A: How old is he?

   B: He's seven.

2. A: How old are they?

   B: They're three.

3. A: _____?

   B: _____ thirteen.

4. A: _____?

   B: _____ ten .

5. A: _____?

   B: _____ seventeen.

6. A: _____?

   B: _____ eighteen.

LISTENING

6. 🔲 **Listen and number the pictures.**

WRITING

7. Fill in the blanks to complete the dialogs.

1. A: Are they four?

   B: No, they aren't.

   A: How old are they?

   B: They're six.

2. A: Are _____ twelve?

   B: No, they aren't.

   A: How old _____ _____?

   B: _____ ten.

3. A: Are they six?

   B: No, _____ _____.

   A: How old _____ _____?

   B: _____ four.

4. A: Is she seven?

   B: No, she isn't.

   A: How old _____ _____?

   B: _____ eight.

5. A: Is _____ sixteen?

   B: No, he isn't.

   A: How old _____ _____ ?

   B: _____ fifteen.

6. A: Is she nine?

   B: No, _____ _____.

   A: How old _____ _____?

   B: _____ ten.

READING

8. Read the page from Cathy's diary.

9. Match the columns.

1. Cathy is   a. sixteen
2. Bill is   b. twelve
3. Juan is   c. thirteen
4. Phil is   d. eleven

10. Answer the questions.

1. How old is Cathy?
She's twelve.

2. How old is Phil?

3. Are Cathy and Hiroshi twelve?

4. How old are Hiroshi and Mariana?

5. Is Mariana thirteen?

DIARY

Dear Diary,
Today is a special day. Today is my birthday. I'm twelve! My friends Hiroshi and Mariana are twelve, too.
Bill is thirteen. Juan is eleven. My brother Phil is sixteen. He's old!!!
Love from Cathy

Look what you know!

GRAMMAR

VERB to be

AFFIRMATIVE	NEGATIVE	QUESTION
I'm (I am)	I'm not (I am not)	Am I ...?
you're (you are)	you're not (you are not)	Are you ...?
he's (he is)	he isn't (he is not)	Is he ...?
she's (she is)	she isn't (she is not)	Is she ...?
we're (we are)	we aren't (we are not)	Are we ...?
you're (you are)	you aren't (you are not)	Are you ...?
they're (they are)	they aren't (they are not)	Are they ...?

PERSONAL PRONOUN
they   They are six.

QUESTION	ANSWER
How old are you?	I'm twelve.

WORD BANK

numbers:
one – twenty
today
birthday

EXTRA!

LEARN SOME WORDS

1. Translate these words. Then find them in the picture below.

mountain bike   roller blades   camera   computer game   present   new   TV

READ SOME MORE

2. Find Sheila's and Terri's presents. Write S or T.

Hi! We're Sheila and Terri. Today is our birthday. We're sisters. We're fourteen. Look! Our birthday presents.

Hi! I'm Sheila. Look! My birthday presents. My new T-shirt, my new computer game, and my new roller blades.

Hi! I'm Terri. Look! My new TV, my new mountain bike, and my new camera!

LISTEN IN

3. Listen and number the pictures.

Katy Jones, New York, twelve, it's my birthday today!

Katy Smith, New York, twelve, it's not my birthday today.

A.

C.

B.

D.

Katie Brown, Los Angeles, twelve, it's not my birthday today.

Katie Green, Los Angeles, thirteen, it's not my birthday today.

NOW YOU'RE TALKING!

4. Talk to another student. Talk to your teacher.

Are you sixteen?   How old are you?

How old is she?   How old is he?

Is she twelve?   Is he fourteen?

41

UNIT
6

They're tall and thin.

1. Listen and practice.

A.
MARIANA: Are they your sisters?
   JUAN: Yes, they are.
MARIANA: They're tall.
   JUAN: Yes, they're tall and thin.

B.
MARIANA: Is your brother tall, too?
   JUAN: Yes, he is.
MARIANA: Is he thin?
   JUAN: Yes, he's tall and thin. Look!

 SPEAKING

2. Listen and practice.

1. She's short.
2. He's tall.

3. He's heavy.

4. They're thin.

SPEAKING

3. **Look at the pictures and practice the dialogs.**

1. A: Is she tall?

   B: No, she isn't.

   She's short.

2. A: Is he short?

   B: No, _____ _____.

   He's _____.

3. A: _____ _____ tall?

   B: _____ _____ _____.

   _____ _____.

4. A: _____ _____ _____.

   B: _____ _____ _____.

   _____ _____.

5. A: _____ _____ _____.

   B: _____ _____ _____.

   _____ _____.

6. A: _____ _____ _____.

   B: _____ _____ _____.

   _____ _____.

4. **Look at the pictures above and describe the people.**

| and | _____ |

Example:
1. She's short and thin.

5. Read and practice.

my	_____
your	_____
his	_____
her	_____
our	_____
their	_____

1. My hair is short.

2. Your hair is short.

3. His hair is long.

4. Her hair is long.

5. Our hair is short.

6. Their hair is long.

WRITING

6. Write about the people on page 43.

1. She is _short_ and _thin_. Her hair is _long_.

2. He is _____ and _____. His hair is _____.

3. He is _____ and _____. His hair is _____.

4. She is _____ and _____. Her hair is _____.

5. He is _____ and _____. His hair is _____.

6. She is _____ and _____. Her hair is _____.

LISTENING

7. 📼 **Listen and number the pictures.**

A.

B. *1*

C.

D.

E.

F.

READING

8. Read and identify the people. Write their names in the boxes.

> This is my band. Alex is short and heavy. His hair is short. Willy is short and heavy, too. His hair is long. Mandy is short and thin. Susan is tall and thin.
>
> I'm tall and thin, too. My hair is long. My name is Jason.

Willy

9. True or False?

| boy | _____ |
| girl | _____ |

1. One girl is tall. *True*

2. Three boys are short. _____

3. Two girls are short. _____

4. Two boys are short and heavy. _____

5. One girl is tall and thin. _____

6. One boy is short and thin. _____

Look what you know!

GRAMMAR

PERSONAL PRONOUNS	POSSESSIVE ADJECTIVES
I	my
you	your
he	his
she	her
we	our
they	their

CONNECTING WORD

and   She's short and thin.

WORD BANK

tall
short
heavy
thin
long
hair
boy
girl

EXTRA!

LEARN SOME WORDS

1. Translate these words. Then find them in the picture below.

guitar   guitarist   bass guitar   bass guitarist   keyboard   keyboard player
drums   drummer   microphone   singer

READ SOME MORE

2. Read and match.

Hi! I'm Rickie. I'm the singer. This is my microphone.

Hi! I'm Tony. I'm the drummer. I play the drums.

Hi! I'm Tina. I'm the keyboard player. I play the keyboard.

Hi! I'm Fred. I'm the bass guitarist. I play the bass guitar.

Hi! I'm Dave. I'm the guitarist. I play the guitar.

LISTEN IN

3. ▭ **Listen and draw the band.**

4. Talk about your favorite group or band.

5. Describe yourself and your brother, sister, or friend.

NOW YOU'RE TALKING!

6. Talk to another student. Talk to your teacher.

　Are you tall?
　How old is your brother?
　Is your brother short?
　Is your brother's hair long?

　Is your hair long?
　How old is your sister?
　Is your sister tall?

REVIEW
UNITS 5-6

1. Write the numbers.

1. 18 _eighteen_

2. 6 _____

3. 1 _____

4. 3 _____

5. 11 _____

6. 5 _____

7. 15 _____

8. 4 _____

9. 8 _____

10. 16 _____

11. 10 _____

12. 14 _____

13. 7 _____

14. 19 _____

15. 17 _____

16. 12 _____

17. 20 _____

18. 2 _____

19. 13 _____

20. 9 _____

2. Fill in the blanks to complete the dialogs.

1. A: Is she ten?

   B: Yes, _she_ _is_.

2. A: Are they eleven?

   B: No, _____ _____.

   A: How old _____ _____?

   B: _____ twelve.

3. A: Is she two?

   B: No, _____ _____.

   A: How old _____ _____ ?

   B: _____ three.

4. A: Are they fourteen?

   B: Yes, _____ _____.

5. A: Is he eight?

   B: No, _____ _____.

   A: How old _____ _____?

   B: _____ nine.

6. A: Are they fifteen?

   B: No, _____ _____.

   A: How old _____ _____?

   B: _____ sixteen.

3. Follow the pattern to write the numbers.

1. **5, 10,** _15_ , _20_ .

2. **2, 4, 6,** _____, _____, _____, _____, _____, _____, _____ .

3. **10, 9, 8,** _____, _____, _____, _____, _____, _____, _____ .

4. **1, 3, 5,** _____, _____, _____, _____, _____, _____, _____ .

4. Look at the pictures and describe the people.

1. *Her name is Ellen.*
   She's tall and thin.
   Her hair is long.

2. _____ Freddie.

   _____

   _____

3. _____ Sue.

   _____

   _____

4. _____ Wendy.

   _____

   _____

5. Match the columns.

1. I'm tall.   a. Their hair is long.

2. You're heavy.   b. My hair is short.

3. He's thin.   c. Our hair is long.

4. She's tall.   d. Your hair is long.

5. They're thin.   e. Her hair is short.

6. We're short.   f. His hair is long.

Now you're ready for the test!

UNIT
7

What's this?

1. 📼 **Listen and practice.**

A.

CATHY: Let's play Crazy Pictures!
BILL: Good idea.
CATHY: What's this?
HIROSHI: Is it a ball?
CATHY: No, it isn't.
BILL: What is it?
CATHY: It's a pencil.

B.

HIROSHI: It's my turn now. What's this?
CATHY: Is it a window?
HIROSHI: No, it isn't.
BILL: Is it a door?
HIROSHI: No, it isn't.
CATHY: What is it?
HIROSHI: It's a desk.

C.

BILL: It's my turn now. What's this?
CATHY: Is it a book?
BILL: No, it isn't.
HIROSHI: Is it a notebook?
BILL: No, it isn't.
CATHY: What is it?
BILL: It's a pen.
HIROSHI: A pen?!
BILL: Yes . . . in a bag.

| it | _____ |

SPEAKING

2. 🔲 **Listen and practice.**

1. pen   2. pencil   3. book   4. pencil sharpener

5. ruler   6. notebook   7. door   8. ball

9. window   10. desk   11. chair   12. bed

3. Look at the pictures above and practice like this.

a	_____

What's this?   It's a pen.

4. Look at the pictures again and practice the dialog.
   Example:
   1. A: Is it a ball?
      B: No, it isn't.
      A: What is it?
      B: It's a pen.

 SPEAKING

5. Read and practice.

This is a pen.

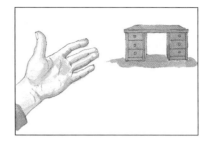

That is a desk.

6. Look at the pictures and practice the dialogs.

this	_____
that	_____

1. A: What's this?

   B: It's a ruler.

2. A: What's that?

   B: It's a bed.

3. A: What's _____?

   B: It's a _____.

4. A: What's _____?

   B: It's a _____.

5. A: What's _____?

   B: _____ _____ _____.

6. A: _____ _____?

   B: _____ _____ _____.

 LISTENING

7. 🎞 **Listen and number the pictures.**

A.

B.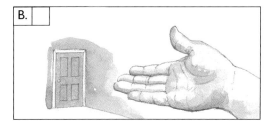

C.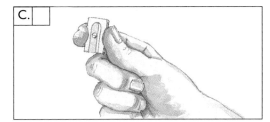

D.

E.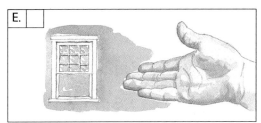

F.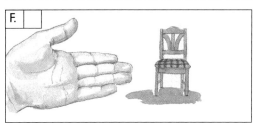

G. *1*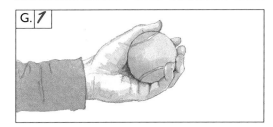

H.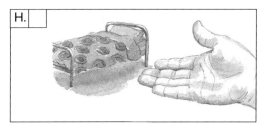

 WRITING

8. Write sentences about the pictures above.

A. *This is a pen.* _____

B. *That is a door.* _____

C. _____

D. _____

E. _____

F. _____

G. _____

H. _____

 READING

9. **Read about Juan and his friends.**

My name is Juan. This is my desk at school. This is my pen and this is my ruler.

That is my friend Ed. He's short. His hair is short, too. That is his pencil and that is his notebook.

That is my friend Carol. She's tall and thin. Her hair is long. That is her book and that is her pencil sharpener.

10. **Match the belongings.**

1. Juan   a. book
         b. pen
2. Ed   c. pencil sharpener
         d. pencil
3. Carol   e. notebook
         f. ruler

11. **Write about your desk and your friends. Use *this* and *that*.**

My name's . . .

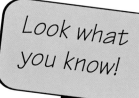

Look what you know!

GRAMMAR	WORD BANK
PERSONAL PRONOUN it	pen desk pencil chair
DEMONSTRATIVE PRONOUNS this that	book bed pencil sharpener ruler
INDEFINITE ARTICLE a	notebook door

QUESTIONS   **ANSWER**

What's this? / that?   It's a pen.

ball
window

LEARN SOME WORDS

1. Check the meaning of these words.

motorcycle   scooter   car   tractor   bus   big   small   fast · slow

READ SOME MORE

2. Match the people to their vehicles.

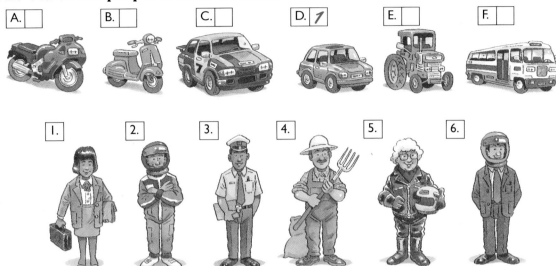

3. Read and check your answers.

1. This is my car. It's small and slow. It's old.

2. This is my car. It's big and fast. It's new.

3. This is my bus. It's big and fast. It's new.

4. This is my tractor. It's big and slow. It's old.

5. This is my motorcycle. Yes, really! It's big and fast. It's new.

6. This is my scooter. It's small and slow. It's old.

4. Write about your bicycle and your family car. Draw a picture.

LISTEN IN

5. ▭ **Listen and write the words.**

1. *bag*   2. _____   3. _____   4. _____

NOW YOU'RE TALKING!

6. Talk to another student. Talk to your teacher.

  Is your hair short?

  What's this?

  Is it a (pencil)?

  What's that?

UNIT
8

Where's my cap?

1. Listen and practice.

A.

BILL: Where's my cap, Debbie?
DEBBIE: It's on the bed.
BILL: No, it isn't.
DEBBIE: It's under the bed then.

B.

BILL: Mom, where's my cap?
MRS. CARSON: It's on the bed.
BILL: No, it isn't.
MRS. CARSON: Yes, it is. It's on the bed, under the T-shirt.

Where's my cap?	_____

 SPEAKING

2. Listen and practice.

1. T-shirt   2. shirt   3. cap   4. sweater   5. skirt

6. jeans   7. socks   8. shoes   9. shorts   10. sneakers

 SPEAKING

3. Read and practice.

on under	_____ _____

The cap is on the desk.

The cap is under the desk.

4. Look at the picture and practice the dialog.

the	_____

Example:

1. A: Where's the shirt?
   B: It's on the desk.

5. Read and practice.

1.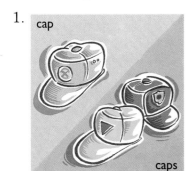
   cap

   caps

2.
   T-shirt

   T-shirts

3.
   sweater

   sweaters

○ ○

6. **Look at the picture and practice like this.**

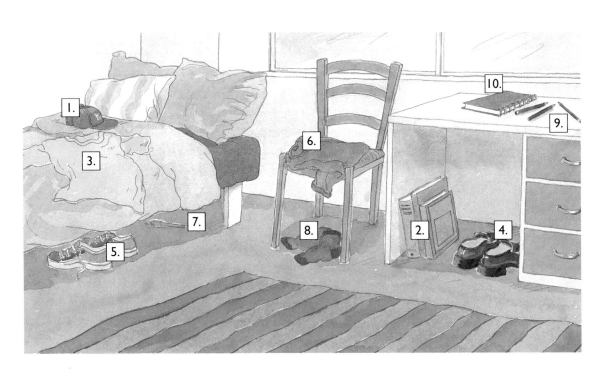

LISTENING

7. 📼 **Look at the picture above. Listen and check True or False.**

	True	False		True	False
1.	✓		6.		
2.			7.		
3.			8.		
4.			9.		
5.			10.		

READING

8. **Read about Bill's room.**

This is my room at home. My notebook is on the chair. My socks are under the chair. Where are my pens?

My ball is on the desk. My book is on the desk, too. My sneakers and my ruler are under the desk.

My caps are on the bed. My shoes are under the bed. Where are my jeans?

9. **Fill in the blanks with *on* or *under*.**

1. His socks are _under_ the chair.

2. His ball is _____ the desk.

3. His book is _____ the desk.

4. His pens are _____ the chair.

5. His jeans are _____ the bed.

WRITING

10. **Answer the questions about Bill's room.**

1. Are his sneakers on the chair?

   No, they aren't. They're under the desk.

2. Is his book under the bed?

   _____

3. Are his socks under the bed?

   _____

4. Is his ruler on the desk?

   _____

5. Are his caps under the chair?

   _____

11. **Write questions for these answers about Bill's room.**

1. *Where are his jeans?*   His jeans are under the bed.

2. _____ His ball is on the desk.

3. _____ His pens are under the chair.

4. _____ His notebook is on the chair.

5. _____ His shoes are under the bed.

Look what you know!

GRAMMAR

PREPOSITIONS
on   The cap is on the bed.
under   The pen is under the chair.

QUESTIONS	ANSWERS
Where's my cap?	It's on the bed.
Where are my caps?	They're on the bed.

PLURAL OF NOUNS
nouns + s:
cap caps   book books
(Some nouns are always plural: *jeans, shorts*.)

DEFINITE ARTICLE
the

WORD BANK

T-shirt	jeans
shirt	socks
cap	shoes
sweater	shorts
skirt	sneakers

LEARN SOME WORDS ➤ **1.** **Check the meaning of these words.**

next to   between   above   below   correct   backpack   question
answer   question mark

READ SOME MORE ➤ **2.** **Read and write the letters in the correct boxes.**

I						
	H		S			
T						
	O	R		E	C	
	N	S		E	R	?

1. Write I between H and S.

2. Write H below H and above O.

3. Write E below I and above R.

4. Write S next to I and above H.

5. Write C below T and next to O.

6. Write R between R and E.

7. Write T below I and next to H.

8. Write A below C and next to N.

9. Write T above the question mark and next to C.

10. Write W between S and E.

LISTEN IN ➤ **3.** **Listen and match.**

NOW YOU'RE TALKING! ➤ **4.** **Talk to another student. Talk to your teacher.**

Where's the (ball)?

Where's my (pen)?

Where are the (books)?

Where are my (shoes)?

REVIEW
UNITS 7-8

I. **Look at the pictures and write the names of these items.**

1. _shoes_

2. _____

3. _____

4. _____

5. _____

6. _____

7. _____

8. _____

9. _____

10. _____

11. _____

12. _____

2. **Write the plurals of these words.**

1. pen _pens_
2. book _____
3. ruler _____
4. notebook _____
5. door _____

6. bed _____
7. shirt _____
8. sweater _____
9. skirt _____
10. cap _____

3. **Look at the picture. Write where things are.**

1. The ball *is under the desk.* _____

2. The pencil _____

3. The shoes _____

4. The T-shirts _____

5. The caps _____

6. The notebook _____

4. **Look at the picture. Write questions for these answers.**

1. *Where are the socks?* _____ The socks are under the desk.

2. _____ The ruler is on the desk.

3. _____ The pens are on the desk.

4. _____ The shorts are on the bed.

5. _____ The book is under the bed.

6. _____ The pencil sharpener is under the chair.

Now you're
ready for
the test!

UNIT

9

What color is it?

1. Listen and practice.

A.

MARIANA: Where's my sweater, Paulo?
PAULO: What color is it?
MARIANA: It's red.
PAULO: It's on the chair.

B.

MARIANA: Where are my shoes?
PAULO: What color are they?
MARIANA: They're red, too.
PAULO: They're in that box.

C.

PAULO: What's your favorite color, Mariana?
MARIANA: Hmmm . . . . My favorite color is blue.
PAULO: No, it isn't. Your favorite color is red!

| What color is it? | _____ |

SPEAKING

2. Listen and practice.

1. blue   2. red   3. yellow   4. green   5. pink

6. gray   7. brown   8. purple   9. black   10. white

3. Practice the dialog like this.

What's your favorite color?

My favorite color is _____.

4. Look at the pictures and practice the dialog.

Example:

1. A: What's this?
   B: It's a pink notebook.

1.

2.

3.

4.

5.

6.

7.

8.

9.

10.

11.

12.

 SPEAKING

5. Look at the picture and practice the dialogs.

| in | _____ |

Example:

1. A: Where is the green notebook?
   B: It's in the box.

2. A: Where are the blue sneakers?
   B: They're under the desk.

WRITING

6. Look at the picture above. Fill in the blanks with a color and *in, on,* or *under.*

1. The *green* notebook is *in* the box.

2. The _____ sneakers are _____ the desk.

3. The _____ pens are _____ the box.

4. The _____ ruler is _____ the desk.

5. The _____ shirt is _____ the desk.

6. The _____ caps are _____ the desk.

7. The _____ pencil sharpener is _____ the box.

8. The _____ shoes are _____ the desk.

 LISTENING

7. 🔲 **Look at the pictures. Listen and check True or False.**

1.

2.

3.

4.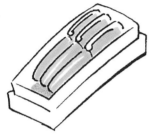

5.

6.

	True	False		True	False
1.		✓	4.		
2.			5.		
3.			6.		

WRITING

8. **Write about the pictures like this.**

1. *The red shirt is in the box.* _____

2. _____

3. _____

4. _____

5. _____

6. _____

READING

9. Read Mariana's postcard.

Dear Aunt Claudia,

How are you? I'm fine. Miami is great. The buildings are blue, pink, yellow, and green.
Cathy is my new friend. Cathy is short and thin. Her hair is short. Her favorite color is purple. My favorite color is red.

Love,
Mariana

10. Fill in the blanks.

1. Mariana is *fine*_____.

2. The houses are blue, pink, _____, and _____.

3. Cathy is short and _____.

4. Cathy's hair is _____.

4. Cathy's favorite color is _____.

5. Mariana's favorite color is _____.

 WRITING

11. Write five sentences about what you are wearing.
My shoes are brown and . . .

Look what you know!

GRAMMAR		WORD BANK		
PREPOSITION		blue	gray	box
in The pencil is in the box.		yellow	purple	
QUESTIONS	**ANSWERS**	red	pink	
What color is it?	It's red.	green	black	
What color is the book?	It's blue.	brown	white	
POSITION OF ADJECTIVES				
The book is blue.				
It's a blue book.				

E X T R A !

LEARN SOME WORDS

1. **Check the meaning of these words.**

school uniform   pants   blouse   tie   jacket   hat

READ SOME MORE

2. **Read about these school uniforms. Number the pictures.**

A. ☐    B. ☐    C. ☐

1. This is my school uniform. The shoes are black. The pants are gray. The shirt is white. The jacket is gray. The tie is red. The cap is gray and red.

2. This is my school uniform. The shoes are black. The skirt is green. The blouse is white. The jacket is green. The tie is blue. The hat is white and green.

3. This is my "school uniform!" The shoes are white and red. The pants are blue. The shirt is red. The jacket is brown. The cap is blue.

3. **Draw your own school uniform. Write about your school uniform.**

LISTEN IN

4. 📼 **Listen and write.**

favorite ↓	1.	2.	you
color	*pink*		
pop group		*Oasis*	
food			
drink	*orange juice*		
sport			

NOW YOU'RE TALKING!

5. **Talk to another student. Talk to your teacher. Talk about your favorite things.**

- What's your favorite color?
- What's your favorite food?
- What's your favorite pop group?
- What color are they?
- What color are your (pants)?
- What's your favorite sport?
- What's your favorite drink?
- What color is it?
- What color is your (bicycle)?

UNIT 10

What's your address?

1. 📼 **Listen and practice.**

A.

MARIANA: What's your address, Bill?
BILL: It's 845 Alpine Road.
MARIANA: Thanks. What's your phone number?
BILL: 555-6073.
MARIANA: I'm sorry. Repeat that, please.
BILL: Five-five-five, six-oh-seven-three.
MARIANA: Thanks.

B.

MARIANA: What's your address, Juan?
JUAN: It's 2106 Valley Avenue.
MARIANA: Thanks. Now, where's Cathy?

 SPEAKING

2. 📼 **Listen and practice.**

21	22	23	24	25
twenty-one	twenty-two	twenty-three	twenty-four	twenty-five

26	27	28	29	30	40
twenty-six	twenty-seven	twenty-eight	twenty-nine	thirty	forty

50	60	70	80	90	100
fifty	sixty	seventy	eighty	ninety	one hundred

SPEAKING

3. 📼 **Listen and practice.**

1.  2.  3.

4. **Look at the cards and practice the dialog.**

What's his address?	_____
What's his phone number?	_____

Example:

1. A: What's his address?
   B: It's seven-thirty-eight Jackson Street.
   A: What's his phone number?
   B: It's five-five-five, seven-oh-five-two.

1.
> John Wong
> 738 Jackson Street
> Miami
> ◆
> PHONE NUMBER:
> 555-7052

2.
> Cindy Jones
> 6413 Park Avenue
> New York
>
> phone number: 555-4356

3.
> *E*dward and *J*ane *J*ordan
> **331 Medford Road**
> **Denver**
> PHONE NUMBER:
> **555-1156**

4.
> ELIZABETH JACKSON
> 1095 MAIN STREET
> CHICAGO
> PHONE NUMBER: 555-9854

5.
> *Robert and Helen Smith*
> *893 Washington Avenue*
> *Washington, D.C.*
> *phone number: 555-7423*

6.
> **Phil Namura**
> **2291 Church Road**
> **Boston**
> **555-6098**

LISTENING

5. Listen and check the correct answer.

1.

A. ✓

Cindy Hall
225 Jackson Street
Denver

B.

Cindy Hall
225 Jackson Avenue
Denver

C.

Cindy Hall
225 Jackson Road
Denver

2.

A.

Name . . . .

. . . .

Phone number 555-8693

B.

Name . . . .

. . . .

Phone number 555-6839

C.

Name . . . .

. . . .

Phone number 555-6893

3.

A.

Carla Lee
609 Maple Street
Chicago

B.

Ted Lee
609 Maple Street
Chicago

C.

Ted and Carla Lee
609 Maple Street
Chicago

4.

A.

B.

C.

5.

A.

B.

C.

 **READING**

6. **Read Mariana's address book.**

Name _Bill Carson_

Address _845 Alpine Road_

Denver

Colorado 80172

Phone number _555-6073_

Name _Juan Diaz_

Address _2106 Valley Avenue_

Los Angeles

California 90136

Phone number _555-6970_

Name _Cathy Hart_

Address _318 Milk Street_

Boston

Massachusetts 02129

Phone number _555-4076_

Name _Hiroshi Ito_

Address _1-9-53 Nishiogikita_

Suginami

Tokyo 167

Phone number _370-5312_

7. **Match the columns.**

1. Bill   a. 2106 Valley Avenue

2. Cathy   b. 845 Alpine Road

3. Juan   c. 1-9-53 Nishiogikita

4. Hiroshi   d. 318 Milk Street

8. **True or False? Are the phone numbers correct?**

1. Bill: five-five-five, six-oh-seven-three   _True_

2. Juan: five-five-five, six-nine-oh-seven   _____

3. Cathy: five-five-five, four-oh-seven-six   _____

4. Hiroshi: three-seven-oh, three-five-one-two   _____

WRITING

9. Write the numbers.

1. **26** *twenty-six*
2. **49** _____
3. **73** _____
4. **85** _____
5. **98** _____

6. **42** _____
7. **33** _____
8. **57** _____
9. **64** _____
10. **79** _____

10. Find and write the numbers. Every line = 100.

32	15	9	A	27
19	35	B	33	5
2	12	49	21	C
23	D	10	4	42
E	17	24	25	10

A = *seventeen* _____
B = _____
C = _____
D = _____
E = _____

11. Write your own address card. Ask each other for addresses and phone numbers.

NAME: ....

ADDRESS: ....

....

PHONE NUMBER: ....

Look what you know!

GRAMMAR

QUESTIONS

What's your | address?
phone number?

WORD BANK

numbers:
twenty-one – one hundred
street
avenue
road

address
phone number

LEARN SOME WORDS

1. Learn these math expressions.

plus +   minus −   divided by ÷   times x   equals =   wrong

READ SOME MORE

2. Answer these math questions.

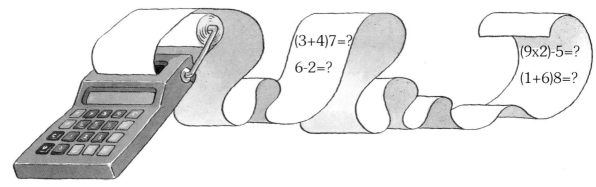

(3+4)7=?
6-2=?

(9x2)-5=?
(1+6)8=?

1. What is five plus nine times four divided by eight? ____

2. What is twenty-seven minus four times nine minus seven divided by two? ____

3. What is sixteen plus eight times five divided by three? ____

4. What is eleven minus three times six minus six divided by seven? ____

3. Write your own math puzzle. Ask a friend to answer.

LISTEN IN

4. ▭ Listen and write.

1.

Name _Bob Green_

Age ____

Address ____

____

Telephone ____

2.

Name _Tina Hart_

Age ____

Address ____

____

Telephone ____

3.

Name _Betty Brown_

Age ____

Address ____

____

Telephone ____

5. Ask another student for the same information.

NOW YOU'RE TALKING!

6. Talk to another student. Talk to your teacher.

▪ What's your address?   ▪ What's your telephone number?
▪ What's his address?   ▪ What's her phone number?
▪ What's their address?   ▪ Could you repeat that?

REVIEW
UNITS 9-10

I. Write sentences about the pictures. Use *in, on,* or *under.*

1.

2.

3.

4.

5.

6.

7.

8.

9.

1. *The green ball is in the box.* _____
2. _____
3. _____
4. _____
5. _____
6. _____
7. _____
8. _____
9. _____

2. Write the numbers.

1. **16** *sixteen*   6. **37** _____   11. **68** _____

2. **29** _____   7. **53** _____   12. **46** _____

3. **99** _____   8. **12** _____   13. **75** _____

4. **81** _____   9. **13** _____   14. **23** _____

5. **10** _____   10. **67** _____   15. **54** _____

3. Look at the picture and answer the questions.

1. What color are her shoes?
   Her shoes are black. _____

2. What color is her cap?
   _____

3. What color is her blouse?
   _____

4. What color is her skirt?
   _____

5. What color is her sweater?
   _____

6. What color are her socks?
   _____

4. Write questions for these answers.

1. *What's his address?* _____   His address is 1691 Jackson Avenue.

2. _____   Her phone number is 323-4996.

3. _____   He's ninety-one.

4. _____   They're twenty-five.

5. _____   My favorite color is pink.

Now you're ready for the test!

Is she an artist?

1. 📼 **Listen and practice.**

A.
JUAN: Who's that woman?
CATHY: That's Cindy Crawford.
JUAN: Cindy Crawford? Is she an artist?
CATHY: No, she isn't.
JUAN: Is she an actor?
CATHY: No!! She's a very famous model!

B.
JUAN: Look, Bill. That's Cindy Crawford.
BILL: Cindy Crawford? Is she a teacher?
JUAN: A teacher? No! She's a very famous model!

 SPEAKING

2. 📼 **Listen and practice.**

a teacher	**an a**ctor	_____

1. an actor

2. an artist

3. an architect

4. an electrician

5. a teacher

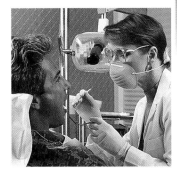
6. a dentist

7. a model

8. a police officer

9. a plumber

10. a taxi driver

11. a farmer

12. a doctor

3. **Look at the pictures on pages 78 and 79 and practice like this.**

She's an artist.

He's a teacher.

4. **Look at the pictures and practice the dialogs.**

Examples:

1. A: Is he a model?
   B: No, he isn't. He's an actor.

2. A: Is she a teacher?
   B: No, she isn't. She's an artist.

WRITING

5. Fill in the blanks with *a* or *an*.

1. *an* electrician

2. _____ teacher

3. _____ doctor

4. _____ artist

5. _____ farmer

6. _____ actor

6. Write about the pictures.

1. He's a dentist.

2. They're actors.

3. _____

4. _____

5. _____

6. _____

7. _____

8. _____

9. _____

7. **Write the plurals of these words.**

1. teacher _teachers_
2. doctor _____
3. model _____
4. actor _____
5. farmer _____

6. artist _____
7. architect _____
8. electrician _____
9. dentist _____
10. plumber _____

 LISTENING

8. Listen and check the correct picture.

1.
 A.
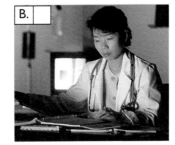 B.
 C. ✔

2.
 A.
 B.
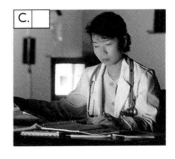 C.

3.
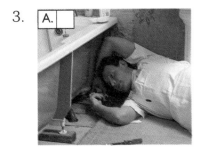 A.
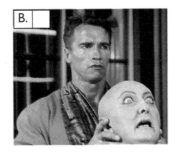 B.
 C.

4.
 A.
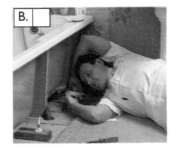 B.
 C.

 READING

9. Read about Juan's family.

Hi! My name is Juan Diaz. This is my father. His name's Carlos Diaz. He's tall and thin, and his hair is black. He's a dentist.

This is my mother. Her name is Gloria Diaz. She's tall and her hair is brown. She's an artist.

This is my brother Diego. He's fourteen.

Ana and Teresa are my sisters. Ana is sixteen and Teresa is eighteen.

10. True or False?

1. Juan's father is tall and heavy.   _False_

2. Carlos Diaz is a dentist.   _____

3. Juan's mother is short.   _____

4. Gloria Diaz is an artist.   _____

5. Carlos is Juan's brother.   _____

6. Diego is fourteen.   _____

7. Ana and Teresa are Juan's sisters.   _____

8. Teresa is twenty-five.   _____

11. Write six sentences about three people in your family.
Marco is my father. He's ...

Look what you know!

GRAMMAR

INDEFINITE ARTICLES

BEFORE CONSONANTS
a   a teacher

BEFORE VOWELS
an   an artist

QUESTION
Is she an artist?

ANSWERS
Yes, she is.
No, she isn't.

WORD BANK

actor	model
artist	police officer
architect	plumber
electrician	taxi driver
teacher	farmer
dentist	doctor

LEARN SOME WORDS

1. Check the meaning of these words.

clothes   students   police station   fashion show   teacher   uniform
criminals   sick   place   job

2. Use the words to complete the chart.

job name	*uniform*	place	job
		school	teaches _____
police officer	blue uniform		catches _____
doctor	white coat	hospital	helps _____ people
model	no		models _____

READ SOME MORE

3. Read about the people. Number the pictures.

A. *4*   B. [ ]   C. [ ]   D. [ ]

1. This is Emma. She's a doctor. She works at Washington Hospital in Boston.
   She helps sick people. She wears a white coat.

2. This is Barry. He's a model. He works at fashion shows in the U.S.A.
   He models clothes. He wears the latest fashion.

3. This is Sally. She's a police officer. She works at the Central Police Station in
   Denver. She catches criminals. She wears a blue police uniform.

4. This is Bob. He's a teacher. He works at Garfield High School in Seattle. He
   teaches students aged 14-17. He wears pants, a shirt, a tie, and a sports jacket.

4. Talk with a friend about your mothers' and fathers' jobs.

LISTEN
IN

5. 🎞 Listen and write.

What's her name?	*Ann Wilmot*
What's her nickname?	
Where is she from?	
What is her job?	
What is her address?	
Is she happy?	
What's her favorite color?	
What's her favorite food?	
What's her favorite group?	
What's her favorite sport?	
What's this? 🏸	

NOW YOU'RE
TALKING!

6. Draw a person. Talk to another student. Talk to your teacher. Use the questions in exercise 5 and the questions below.
- Is he a teacher?
- Is she a model?
- What's his job?
- What's her job?

Where's he from?

1. 📼 **Listen and practice.**

A.

MARIANA: Who's this man?

HIROSHI: His name's Danny DeVito. He's an actor.

MARIANA: Where's he from?

HIROSHI: He's from the United States. He's American.

B.

MARIANA: Hiroshi, look! That's Danny DeVito.

HIROSHI: No, it isn't. Danny DeVito is short. That man's tall.

C.

MARIANA: Excuse me. Are you Danny DeVito?

MAN: No, I'm not. My name's Charlie Baker.

MARIANA: Oh, I'm sorry!

 SPEAKING

2. Read and practice.

A: Who's this man?
B: His name's Danny DeVito.

A: Who's this woman?
B: Her name's Cindy Crawford.

SPEAKING

3. Listen and practice.

4. Michael Jordan
American

UNITED STATES

5. David Hockney
English

MEXICO

3. Luis Miguel
Mexican

BRAZIL

2. Rubens Barichello
Brazilian

ARGENTINA

1. Gabriella Sabatini
Argentinian

4. **Look at the pictures and practice the dialogs.**
Example:
1. A: Who's this woman?
   B: Her name's Gabriella Sabatini.
2. A: Who's this man?
   B: His name's Rubens Barichello.

5. **Look at the pictures and practice the dialogs.**
Example:
1. A: Where's she from?
   B: She's from Argentina. She's Argentinian.
2. A: Where's he from?
   B: He's from Brazil. He's Brazilian.

6. Claudia Schiffer
German

7. Gong Li
Chinese

8. Mitsuko Uchida
Japanese

ENGLAND

GERMANY

SPAIN

CHINA

JAPAN

10. Joaquín Cortés
Spanish

AUSTRALIA

9. Mel Gibson
Australian

WRITING

6. Fill in the blanks.

1. She's from *Argentina*. She's *Argentinian*.

2. He's from _____. He's _____.

3. He's from _____. He's _____.

4. He's from the _____. He's _____.

5. He's from _____. He's _____.

6. She's from _____. She's _____.

7. She's from _____. She's _____.

8. She's from _____. She's _____.

9. He's from _____. He's _____.

10. He's from _____. He's _____.

LISTENING

7. Listen and number the pictures.

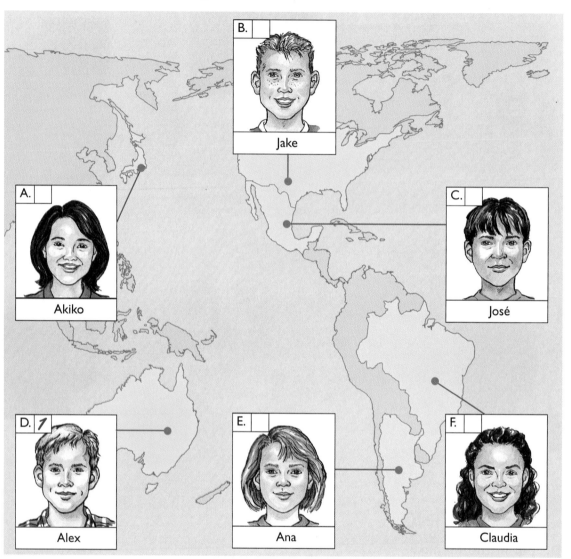

WRITING

8. Write sentences about the people above.

1. *He's from Australia. He's Australian.*

2. _____

3. _____

4. _____

5. _____

6. _____

READING

9. **Read about the famous people.**

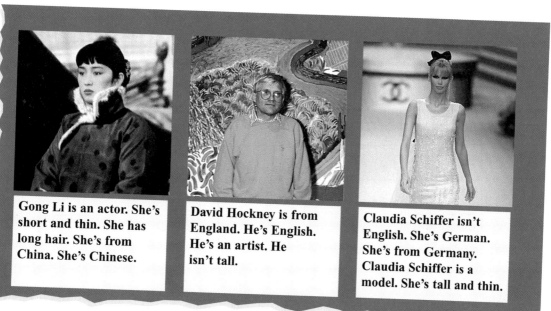

Gong Li is an actor. She's short and thin. She has long hair. She's from China. She's Chinese.

David Hockney is from England. He's English. He's an artist. He isn't tall.

Claudia Schiffer isn't English. She's German. She's from Germany. Claudia Schiffer is a model. She's tall and thin.

10. **Answer the questions.**

1. Where's Gong Li from?

    She's from China.

2. Is she an artist?

    _____

3. Where's David Hockney from?

    _____

4. Is he an actor?

    _____

5. Is Claudia Schiffer English?

    _____

6. Is she short and heavy?

    _____

Look what you know!

GRAMMAR	
QUESTIONS	
Who's (who is)	this man? / that woman?
Where's (where is)	he / she from?

WORD BANK		
Mexico/Mexican	Argentina/Argentinian	man
Spain/Spanish	Brazil/Brazilian	woman
Germany/German	England/English	
Japan/Japanese	U.S.A./American	
China/Chinese	Australia/Australian	

⭕⭕⭕⭕⭕Ⓔ Ⓧ Ⓣ Ⓡ Ⓐ ❗⭕⭕⭕⭕

LEARN SOME WORDS ▷ **1. Check the meaning of these words.**

language   capital   city   continent   nationality   North America
South America   Europe   Africa   Asia   Australasia   speak

READ SOME MORE ▷ **2. Read. Then guess the country. Write in the chart.**

	1.	2.	3.	4.
country				*Belgium*
capital	*Ottawa*			
languages				
nationality				
continent				

1. This is a big country. The people speak English and French. The country
is in North America. The capital is Ottawa. The country is called _____.
The people are _____.

2. This is a small country. The people speak Chinese, Malay, Tamil, and English.
The country is in Asia. The capital is Singapore City. The country is
called _____. The people are _____.

3. This is a big country. The people speak Portuguese. The country is in South
America. The capital is Brasilia. The country is called _____.
The people are _____.

4. This is a small country. The people speak French, Dutch, and German.
The country is in Europe. The capital is Brussels. The country is called _____.
The people are _____.

3. Write about your country.

**4. Look at the map of the world on pages 86-87. Talk about other countries,
nationalities, languages, and cities.**

E X T R A !

5. Look at the flags. Name the countries.

A. *Turkey*

B.

C.

D.

E.

F.

G.

H.

LISTEN IN

6. 🎦 Listen and write the country, nationality, and language.

	1.	2.	3.
country	*Turkey*		
nationality		*Russian*	
language			

NOW YOU'RE TALKING!

7. Look at pages 86 and 87. Talk to another student. Talk to your teacher.

- Who's this man?
- Who's this woman?
- Where is he from?
- What nationality is she?
- What are their names?
- Where are they from?
- What nationality are they?
- What nationality are you?

REVIEW
UNITS 11-12

1. **Fill in the blanks with *a* or *an*.**

1. *a*____ taxi driver
2. _____ electrician
3. _____ artist
4. _____ farmer
5. _____ police officer
6. _____ actor

2. **Look at the pictures and write the name of each profession.**

1. *doctor*_____   2. _____   3. _____

4. _____   5. _____   6. _____

7. _____   8. _____   9. _____

3. Look at the pictures and write about the people.

1. *Her name's Cathy.*
   She's from the United States.
   She's American.

2. _____
   _____
   _____

3. _____
   _____
   _____

4. _____
   _____
   _____

4. Fill in the blanks with the correct nationality.

1. He's from China. He's *Chinese* _____.

2. We're from Spain. We're _____.

3. I'm from Mexico. I'm _____.

4. They're from England. They're _____.

5. You're from Australia. You're _____.

6. She's from Argentina. She's _____.

5. Match the opposites.

1. boy   a. man

2. black   b. short

3. tall   c. girl

4. heavy   d. thin

5. woman   e. white

Now you're ready for the test!

UNIT
13

What's the weather like?

1. 🔊 **Listen and practice.**

A.
MRS. HART: What's the weather like on Seashell Island?
MAN: It's sunny.
MRS. HART: Is it hot in August?
MAN: Yes, it's sunny and hot.
MRS. HART: Great! Three tickets to Seashell Island, please.
MAN: Here you are.
MRS. HART: Thank you.

B.
CATHY: Mom, the weather is rainy on Seashell Island!
JANET: It's not hot, either! It's cool.
MRS. HART: Maybe it's sunny and hot in January!
CATHY: Too bad it's August!

SPEAKING

2. 🎧 **Listen and practice.**

rainy   sunny   windy   cloudy   snowy

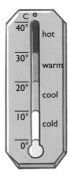

3. **Practice the dialog like this.**

| What's the weather like? | _____ |

 What's the weather like?

 It's rainy.

4. **Look at the pictures in exercise 2 and practice the dialogs.**
Example:
A: Is it cool today?
B: Yes, it's cool and rainy.

5. 🎧 **Listen and practice.**

JANUARY   **FEBRUARY**   **MARCH**   **APRIL**

MAY   **JUNE**   **JULY**   **AUGUST**

SEPTEMBER   **OCTOBER**   **NOVEMBER**   **DECEMBER**

SPEAKING

6. **Look at the calendar and practice the dialog.**

| in | ____ |

Example:
A: What's the weather like in January?
B: It's cold and rainy in January.

7. **Look at the calendar and practice the dialog.**
Example:
A: Is it hot in January?
B: No, it isn't. It's cold in January.

WRITING

8. Look at the weather information and write about the cities.

The temperature is 13°C.	_____

THE WEATHER TODAY IN THE U.S.A.

1.	Boston		13°C
2.	Los Angeles		22°C
3.	New York		12°C
4.	Denver		0°C
5.	Miami		31°C
6.	Chicago		5°C

C
40° hot
30° warm
20° cool
10° cold
0°

1. *It's rainy and cool in Boston. The temperature is 13°C.*

2. _____

3. _____

4. _____

5. _____

6. _____

LISTENING

9. Listen and number the pictures.

A. *1*   B.   C.   D.

 READING

10. Read about the weather.

The Weather Today

- It's sunny in Miami today. The temperature is 22°C.
- It's warm in Tokyo, too. It's sunny and windy in Tokyo.
- In São Paulo the weather is cloudy and the temperature is 15°C.
- It's snowy in Moscow and the temperature is 2°C.
- It's cold in Buenos Aires, too. It's cold and very windy.

11. True or False?

1. It's cold and rainy in Miami.   *False*

2. It's windy and warm in Tokyo.   _____

3. It's sunny in Miami and Tokyo.   _____

4. It's hot in São Paulo.   _____

5. It's windy in Tokyo and Buenos Aires.   _____

6. It isn't sunny in São Paulo.   _____

7. It's rainy and cold in Moscow.   _____

8. The temperature in Moscow is 2°C.   _____

Look what you know!

12. Write about the weather in your city. Follow the pattern for March, June, and September.

It's warm and rainy in January.

GRAMMAR		WORD BANK			
QUESTION	**ANSWER**	sunny	hot	January	July
What's the weather like?	It's sunny.	rainy	warm	February	August
		snowy	cool	March	September
PREPOSITION		cloudy	cold	April	October
in	What's the weather like in March?	windy		May	November
		temperature		June	December

LEARN SOME WORDS

1. Check the meaning of these words and expressions.

skiing   hiking   swimming   having a barbecue   reading a book
watching a movie   playing soccer   playing tennis

READ SOME MORE

2. Look at the chart and read the description.

Example:

It's cold and snowy in Nagano, Japan in January. The temperature
is about 0 degrees. It's a great month for skiing!

	1.	2.	3.	4.
city	Nagano	Seoul	Mexico City	London
country	Japan	Korea	Mexico	England
month	January	March	September	November
temperature	0 degrees	10 degrees	20 degrees	10 degrees
weather	cold and snowy	cool and sunny	warm and sunny	cool and rainy
sport/activity	skiing	hiking	having a barbecue	reading a book watching a movie

3. Write descriptions for the other three places on the chart.

4. Write a description for your own city or area.

5. 🖭 **Listen and circle the number you hear.**

1. 13 (30)

2. 14 40

3. 15 50

4. 16 60

5. 17 70

6. 18 80

7. 19 90

8. 5   9

6. 🖭 **Listen and write the missing numbers.**

1. The temperature today is _13_ degrees Celsius.

2. She's _____ years old.

3. The temperature in the Sudan in July is _____ degrees Celsius.

4. He lives at _____ Park Avenue.

5. He's _____ years old.

6. She lives at _____ Main Street.

7. My lucky number is _____.

8. She's _____ years old today!

9. This is unit _____.

10. Please turn to page _____.

7. **Talk to another student. Talk to your teacher.**

▨ What's the weather like today?

▨ What's the weather like in March?

▨ Is it hot in January?

▨ Is it cool in April?

▨ Is it cold in August?

▨ Is it warm in November?

▨ What's the weather like in London today?

▨ What's the weather like in Tokyo in March?

What are these?

1. 🔊 **Listen and practice.**

A.

MARIANA: What are these animals?
JUAN: They're kangaroos.
They're from Australia.
HIROSHI: Wow! Look at those!
JUAN: Those are tigers.
MARIANA: Are they from Africa?
JUAN: No, they're from India.

B.

HIROSHI: Where's that bird from, Juan?
JUAN: That bird's from Brazil.
MARIANA: Let's go see it.

C.

HIROSHI: That's your bird from Brazil, Juan!

 SPEAKING

2. 🔊 **Listen and practice.**

1. a zebra   2. an elephant   3. an eagle   4. a giraffe

SPEAKING

3. 🔲 **Listen and practice.**

1. a koala   2. a tiger   3. a kangaroo

4. a panda   5. a toucan   6. a macaw

4. **Look at the picture and practice** *this, that, these,* **and** *those.*

this	_____
these	_____
that	_____
those	_____

This is an eagle.   These are eagles.

That is a kangaroo.   Those are kangaroos.

5. **Look at the picture and practice the dialogs.**

Examples:

A: What's this?   A: What are those?

B: It's a koala.   B: They're pandas.

WRITING

6. **Look at the picture above. Fill in the blanks with *this, that, these,* or *those.***

1. *This* _____ is a tiger.

2. *These* _____ are toucans.

3. _____ is a giraffe.

4. _____ are macaws.

5. _____ are kangaroos.

6. _____ is a zebra.

7. _____ are elephants.

8. _____ is an eagle.

LISTENING

7. 🔲 **Listen and check the correct answers.**

	U.S.A.	China	Australia	Brazil		BIRDS	MAMMALS
1. pandas		✓					✓
2. kangaroos							
3. eagles							
4. toucans							

8. Fill in the blanks.

1. Pandas are from _China_.   They are _Chinese_ _mammals_.

2. Kangaroos are from _____.   They are _____ _____.

3. Eagles are from the _____.   They are _____ _____.

4. Toucans are from _____.   They are _____ _____.

 READING

9. **Read about the animals.**

These are giraffes. Giraffes are from Africa. They are African mammals. They are very tall and thin. Giraffes are brown and white.

Macaws aren't mammals. They are birds. Macaws are from Brazil. They are red, blue, green, yellow, white, and black!

This is a koala. It is from Australia. It is a mammal. The koala is gray and white. It isn't very tall.

10. **True or False?**

1. Giraffes are birds.   *False*

2. Giraffes are from Africa.   _____

3. The koala is gray and white.   _____

4. Macaws are birds.   _____

5. Macaws are from Australia.   _____

6. The koala is from Africa.   _____

Look what you know!

GRAMMAR

DEMONSTRATIVE PRONOUNS

this	This is a koala.
these	These are toucans.
that	That is a giraffe.
those	Those are pandas.

WORD BANK

giraffe	kangaroo	bird
zebra	panda	mammal
elephant	toucan	animal
koala	eagle	
tiger	macaw	

◯◯◯◯◯(E)(X)(T)(R)(A)(!)◯◯◯◯◯

LEARN SOME WORDS ▷ **1.** **Check the meaning of these words.**
dog   monkey   cat   live   frog   snake   parrot   hummingbird

READ SOME MORE ▷ **2.** **Read the quizzes and circle the correct answers.**

Panda Quiz

1. Pandas are: a. birds. b. mammals. c. dogs. d. monkeys.
2. Pandas are: a. black and white. b. red and yellow.
                                   c. gray and white. d. yellow and brown.
3. Pandas are from: a. South Africa. b. India. c. Brazil. d. China.
4. Pandas live for: a. 10–20 years. b. 20–30 years.
                                   c. 30–40 years. d. 40–50 years.

**Pandas need your help to survive.
Help to save Pandas!**

Tiger Quiz

1. Tigers are: a. birds. b. cats. c. dogs. d. monkeys.
2. Tigers are: a. black and white. b. red and brown.
                                  c. gray and white. d. yellow and brown.
3. Tigers are from: a. South Africa. b. India. c. Brazil. d. China.
4. Tigers live for: a. 10–15 years. b. 15–20 years.
                                  c. 20–30 years. d. 30–40 years.

**Tigers need your help to survive.
Help to save Tigers!**

106

LISTEN
IN

3. 📷 **Listen and number the pictures.**

A. *1*

B.

C.

D.

4. Guess the animal.
It's gray.   It's big.   It's long.   It swims.   It's not a fish.

NOW YOU'RE
TALKING!
**5. Talk to another student. Talk to your teacher. Look at the pictures
in Unit 14. Ask questions and point to the pictures.**

  What's this?
  What are these?
  What's that?
  What are those?
  Is this a (panda)?
  Are these (toucans)?
  Is that a (giraffe)?
  Are those (koalas)?
  Where's that (bird) from?
  Where's that (animal) from?

REVIEW
UNITS 13-14

1. **Look at the picture and fill in the blanks with** *this, that, these,* **or** *those.*

1. *This* _____ is an elephant.
2. _____ is a macaw.
3. _____ is a toucan.
4. _____ are kangaroos.
5. _____ is a zebra.

6. _____ are koalas.
7. _____ is a panda.
8. _____ are tigers.
9. _____ is an eagle.
10. _____ are giraffes.

2. **Look at the picture and write questions and answers.**

1. *What's that?*
   It's a zebra.
2. *What are these?*
   They're giraffes.
3. _____
   _____
4. _____
   _____
5. _____
   _____

6. _____
   _____
7. _____
   _____
8. _____
   _____
9. _____
   _____
10. _____
   _____

3. Look at the weather information and write about the cities.

THE WEATHER TODAY AROUND THE WORLD

1.	Tokyo		8°C
2.	São Paulo		24°C
3.	London		12°C
4.	Boston		2°C
5.	Miami		31°C
6.	New York City		15°C
7.	Buenos Aires		32°C
8.	Moscow		22°C

C °
40°   hot
30°
        warm
20°
        cool
10°   cold
0°

1. *It's sunny and cold in Tokyo. The temperature is 8°C.*
2. _____
3. _____
4. _____
5. _____
6. _____
7. _____
8. _____

4. Match the columns.

1. What's the weather like?   a. They're from Australia.

2. Is it hot in August?   b. Those are giraffes.

3. What are those animals?   c. It's an elephant.

4. What's this?   d. It's sunny and hot.

5. What are these animals?   e. No, it's cool in August.

6. Where are koalas from?   f. These are tigers.

Now you're ready for the test!

UNIT 15

What time is it?

1. 📼 **Listen and practice.**

A.

MR. ITO: Come on, kids. We're late!
HIROSHI: What time is the baseball game?
MR. ITO: 9 o'clock.
HIROSHI: What time is it now?
MR. ITO: It's 8 o'clock.

B.

HIROSHI: What time is it?
MR. ITO: It's 8:30.
AKIRA: Look, Dad!
MR. ITO: Oh, no. The baseball game is at 9 o'clock. But 9 o'clock in the evening, not 9 o'clock in the morning!

| What time is it? | _____ |

SPEAKING

2. Listen and practice.

1 o'clock

2 o'clock

3 o'clock

4 o'clock

5 o'clock

6 o'clock

7 o'clock

8 o'clock

9 o'clock

10 o'clock

11 o'clock

12 o'clock

3. Practice the dialog like this.

What time is it?

It's 1 o'clock.

4. Look at the pictures and practice the dialog.

Example:

1. A: Is it 2 o'clock?
   B: No, it isn't. It's 3 o'clock.

1.

2.

3.

4.

5.

6.

7.

8.

SPEAKING

5. 🎞 **Listen and practice.**

SUNDAY

 9 A.M.
picnic

MONDAY

 11 A.M.
bike race

TUESDAY

 2 P.M.
English class

WEDNESDAY

 4 P.M.
baseball game

THURSDAY

 5 P.M.
movie

FRIDAY

 6 P.M.
party

SATURDAY

 8 P.M.
concert

6. **Look at the pictures and practice the dialog.**

on	_____	A.M.	_____
at	_____	P.M.	_____

Example:
A: What time is the picnic?
B: It's on Sunday at 9 A.M.

 LISTENING

7. 📼 Listen and check the correct picture.

1. A. ✓ 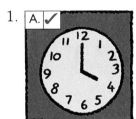　B. 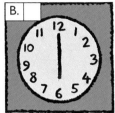　　2. A. 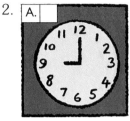　B.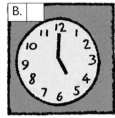

3. A. 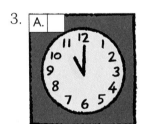　B. 　　4. A.  SUNDAY 9 P.M.　B.  WEDNESDAY 9 P.M.

5. A. 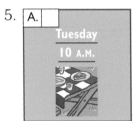 Tuesday 10 A.M.　B.  Thursday 10 A.M.　　6. A. 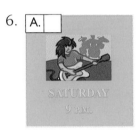 SATURDAY 9 P.M.　B.  Friday 7 P.M.

 WRITING

8. **Look at the pictures above and answer the questions.**

1. A. What time is it? _It's 4 o'clock._____

    B. What time is it? _____

2. A. What time is it? _____

    B. What time is it? _____

3. A. What time is it? _____

    B. What time is it? _____

4. A. What time is the baseball game? _____

    B. What time is the party? _____

5. A. What time is the picnic? _____

    B. What time is the bike race? _____

6. A. What time is the concert? _____

    B. What time is the movie? _____

 READING

9. **Read Hiroshi's note.**

> Sunday: picnic 11 A.M.
> Wednesday: movie 8 P.M.
> Friday: party 8 P.M.
> Saturday: concert 9 P.M.

10. **Look at the note above and fill in Hiroshi's schedule.**

SUNDAY	MONDAY	TUESDAY	WEDNESDAY	THURSDAY	FRIDAY	SATURDAY
	3 P.M. English class	3 P.M. English class		3 P.M. English class		

 WRITING

11. **Look at the schedule above and answer the questions.**

1. What time are his English classes?
   They're at 3 P.M. on Monday, Tuesday, and Thursday.

2. Is the party on Saturday?
   _____

3. What time is the concert?
   _____

4. What time is the movie?
   _____

5. What time is the picnic?
   _____

Look what you know!

GRAMMAR

PREPOSITIONS

on   The picnic is on Monday.
at   The picnic is at 1 o'clock.

QUESTION   **ANSWER**
What time is it?   It's 8 o'clock

WORD BANK

Sunday	Thursday	picnic	class
Monday	Friday	baseball game	concert
Tuesday	Saturday	movie	bike race
Wednesday		party	

●●●●●●E X T R A !●●●●●●●

I. Check the meaning of these words.

event   picnic   theater   meet   outside   message

2. Read Mariana's message. Write messages for the other events.

Example:

Dear Hiroshi,
The movie is today at 7:00 at
West Gate Movie Theater.
Meet me outside the theater
at 6.45.
Mariana

I.
Hiroshi
movie
today
7 P.M.
West Gate Movie Theater
outside theater 6:45
Mariana

2.
Cathy
picnic
Sunday
11 A.M.
Central Park
train station 10 A.M.
Hiroshi

3.
Juan
concert
Saturday
9 P.M.
Eastwood Hall
outside hall 8:45
Janet

4.
Hiroshi
party
Friday
8 P.M.
Bill's house
Bill's house 8 P.M.
Cathy

5.
Mariana
baseball game
Sunday
6 P.M.
Giant's Stadium
outside stadium,
gate 8A, 5:30
Janet

3. ▭ Listen and number the pictures.

A. 1
B.
C.
D.

4. Talk to another student. Talk to your teacher.

What time is it?
Is the (picnic) at (9 o'clock)?
Is the (picnic) on (Monday)?
Are we early?

What time is the (picnic)?
Is the (picnic) today?
Are we late?
Are we on time?

UNIT 16

What's your favorite subject?

1. **Listen and practice.**

A.

MARIANA: What time is it?

JUAN: It's three fifteen.

MARIANA: The space movie is at three thirty.

BILL: I can't wait!

B.

MARIANA: What's your favorite subject?

JUAN: My favorite subject is history. What about you, Bill?

BILL: My favorite subject is math.

What's your favorite subject?	_____

SPEAKING

2. **Listen and practice.**

1. seven oh five   2. seven ten   3. seven fifteen   4. seven twenty-five

5. seven thirty   6. seven forty   7. seven forty-five   8. seven fifty

SPEAKING

3. **Look at the pictures and practice like this.**

 What time is it?

 It's two forty-five.

1.   2. **10:15**   3. **9:40**   4.

5.   6. **7:35**   7.   8.

9. **6:05**   10. **1:55**   11.   12.

 WRITING

4. **Look at the pictures and fill in the blanks.**

1. *seven twenty-five*   2. _____   3. _____

4. _____   5. _____   6. _____

7. _____   8. _____   9. _____

 SPEAKING

5. 📼 **Listen and practice.**

1. biology

2. English

3. math

4. physics

5. history

6. art

7. geography

8. music

9. computer lab

10. physical education

6. **Look at the school schedule and practice the dialog.**

Example:
A: What time is music on Monday?
B: It's at nine ten on Monday.

	MONDAY	TUESDAY	WEDNESDAY	THURSDAY	FRIDAY
7:30	English	physical education	math	physical education	geography
8:20	math	physics	geography	biology	computer lab
9:10	music	biology	art	English	math
10:00	BREAK	BREAK	BREAK	BREAK	BREAK
10.20	computer lab	English	physics	computer lab	art
11:00	history	art	history	music	English

LISTENING

7. 🔊 **Listen and check True or False.**

	True	False
1.	✓	
2.		
3.		
4.		
5.		
6.		
7.		
8.		
9.		
10.		

	MONDAY	TUESDAY
12:15	physical education	geography
1:05	biology	computer lab
1:50	English	physics
2:45	math	art
3:30	music	history

8. 🔊 **Listen and match the columns.**

1. the concert   a. 5:20
2. biology   b. 4:30
3. English   c. 12:00
4. the baseball game   d. 7:00
5. math   e. 6:15
6. geography   f. 10:45
7. the movie   g. 1:25
8. history   h. 2:40
9. the picnic   i. 3:05
10. art   j. 8:10

READING

9. **Read about Mariana and her friends.**

Hi! My name is Mariana. These
are my friends at school. Their
names are Elizabeth and Helen.
My favorite subject is math.
Math is at 9:20 on Monday.
Elizabeth's favorite subject is
history. History is at 10:15 on
Wednesday. Helen's favorite
subject is art. Art is at 2:25 on
Friday.

10. **Answer the questions.**

1. What is Mariana's favorite subject?

   Her favorite subject is math.

2. What is Elizabeth's favorite subject?

   _____

3. What is Helen's favorite subject?

   _____

4. What time is math?

   _____

5. What time is art?

   _____

6. What time is history?

   _____

Look what you know!

GRAMMAR

QUESTION
What's your favorite subject?

ANSWER
My favorite subject is math.

WORD BANK

biology	art	physical education
English	history	computer lab
math	geography	
physics	music	

○○○○○(E)(X)(T)(R)(A)(!)○○○○○○

1. Check the meaning of these words and expressions.

questionnaire   telling the truth   lying

2. Complete this questionnaire.

What's your name? _____	Are you tall? _____
Where are you from? _____	Is your hair long? _____
What nationality are you? _____	Is your hair black? _____
What languages do you speak? _____	What's your father's job? _____
What's your address? _____	What's your mother's job? _____
What's your telephone number? _____	What's your favorite color? _____
When is your birthday? _____	What's your favorite animal? _____
How old are you? _____	What's your favorite subject? _____

3. Ask another student the questions.

4. 🔲 **Listen. Write the man's answers.**

	answer 1	answer 2
name:		
address:		
telephone number:		
birthday:		

Is the man telling the truth or lying?

5. Talk to another student. Talk to your teacher.

What day is it?
What month is it?
What time is English on Monday?
What's your favorite subject?

REVIEW
UNITS 15-16

1. **Look at the pictures and fill in the blanks.**

1. *two o'clock*

2. _____

3. _____

4. _____

5. _____

6. _____

7. _____

8. _____

9. _____

2. **Look at the schedule and answer the questions.**

	MONDAY	TUESDAY	WEDNESDAY	THURSDAY	FRIDAY
7:30	biology	physical education	math	physical education	geography
8:20	math	physics	geography	biology	computer lab
9:10	music	history	art	English	math

1. What time is music on Monday?
   It's at nine ten on Monday.

2. What time is history on Tuesday?

   _____

3. What time is math on Wednesday?

   _____

4. What time is geography on Wednesday?

   _____

5. What time is physical education on Thursday?

   _____

6. What time is computer lab on Friday?

   _____

3. **Look at the posters and write about the events.**

1.

2.

3.

4.

5.

6.

1. _The baseball game is at 7 P.M. on Tuesday._

2. _____

3. _____

4. _____

5. _____

6. _____

4. **Match the columns.**

1. What's your name?
2. How are you?
3. How old is she?
4. What time is it?
5. What time is the picnic?
6. What color is the skirt?
7. Where is the pen?
8. Is he tall?
9. Where are they from?
10. What time is the movie?

a. The movie is at 8 P.M.
b. It's green.
c. My name is John.
d. The picnic is at 5 P.M.
e. The pen is on the desk.
f. No, he isn't.
g. I'm fine, thanks.
h. They're from China.
i. She's twenty-one.
j. It's 10 o'clock.

Now you're ready for the test!

Wordlist

Note: The numbers in parentheses refer to the unit in which the word first appears.

A
a (7)
above (8)
actor (11)
address (10)
Africa (12)
American (12)
an (11)
and (6)
animal (14)
answer (8)
apple pie (4)
April (13)
architect (11)
Argentina (12)
Argentinian (12)
around (14)
art (16)
artist (11)
Asia (12)
at (15)
at home (8)
August (13)
Australasia (12)
Australia (12)
Australian (12)
avenue (10)

B
backpack (7)
ball (7)
band (6)
baseball game (15)
bass guitar (6)
bathroom (3)
bed (7)
bedroom (3)
below (8)
between (8)
big (7)
bike race (15)
biology (16)
bird (14)
birthday (5)
black (9)
blackboard (2)
blouse (9)
blue (9)

body (14)
book (7)
box (9)
boy (6)
Brazil (12)
Brazilian (12)
brother (2)
brown (9)
bus (7)
bye (3)

C
camera (5)
cap (8)
capital (12)
car (7)
cat (14)
chair (2)
China (12)
Chinese (12)
city (12)
class (15)
clock (2)
clothes (11)
cloudy (13)
cold (13)
color (9)
Come on. (15)
computer game (5)
computer lab (16)
concert (15)
continent (12)
cool (13)
correct (8)
criminals (11)

D
day (5)
December (13)
dentist (11)
desk (2)
dining room (3)
divided by (10)
doctor (11)
dog (14)
door (2)
drummer (6)
drums (6)

E
eagle (14)
eight (5)
eighteen (5)
eighty (10)
either (13)
electrician (11)
elephant (14)
eleven (5)
England (12)
English (12)
equals (10)
Europe (12)
event (15)
eyes (14)

F
family (2)
famous (11)
farmer (11)
fashion show (11)
fast (7)
father (2)
favorite (9)
February (13)
fifteen (5)
fifty (10)
fine (4)
first (1)
five (5)
four (5)
forty (10)
fourteen (5)
french fries (4)
Friday (15)
fried chicken (4)
friend (2)
frog (14)

G
garage (3)
geography (16)
German (12)
Germany (12)
giraffe (14)
girl (6)
girlfriend (4)
Good afternoon. (3)

Good evening. (3)
Good morning. (3)
Goodbye (3)
gray (9)
great (9)
Great! (13)
green (9)
guitar (6)
guitarist (6)

H

hair (6)
hamburger (4)
happy (4)
hat (9)
having a barbecue (13)
he (3)
head (14)
heavy (6)
Hello! (1)
her (2)
Here you are. (13)
Hi! (1)
hiking (13)
his (2)
history (16)
home (8)
hot (13)
house (3)
How are you? (4)
How old are you? (5)
hummingbird (4)
hungry (4)

I

I can't wait! (16)
ice cream (4)
I'm sorry. (10)
in (9)
in-line skates (5)
India (14)
is (1)
it (7)

J

jacket (9)
January (13)
Japan (12)
Japanese (12)
jeans (8)
job (11)
July (13)
June (13)

K

kangaroo (14)
keyboard (6)
keyboard player (6)
kids (15)
kitchen (3)
koala (14)

L

language (12)
last (1)
late (15)
launch (16)
legs (14)
live (14)
living room (3)
long (6)
Look. (4)
Love, (5)
lying (16)

M

macaw (14)
mammal (14)
man (12)
March (13)
math (16)
May (13)
me (2)
meet (15)
message (15)
Mexican (12)
Mexico (12)
microphone (6)
middle (1)
minus (10)
model (11)
Monday (15)
mother (2)
motor cycle (7)
mountain bike (5)
mouth (14)
movie (15)
music (16)
my (1)
My name's . . . . (1)

N

nationality (12)
new (5)
next to (8)
Nice to meet you (2)
nickname (2)

nine (5)
nineteen (5)
ninety (10)
North America (12)
notebook (7)
November (13)
now (15)

O

October (13)
old (5)
on (8)
one (5)
one hundred (10)
orange juice (4)
our (6)
outside (15)

P

panda (14)
pants (9)
parrot (14)
party (15)
pen (7)
pencil (7)
pencil sharpener (7)
phone number (10)
physical education (16)
physics (16)
picnic (15)
pink (9)
pizza (4)
place (11)
playing soccer (13)
playing tennis (13)
please (10)
plumber (11)
plus (10)
police officer (11)
police station (11)
present (5)
purple (9)

Q

question (8)
question mark (8)
questionnaire (16)

R

rainy (13)
reading a book (13)
red (9)
repeat (10)

restaurant (4)
road (10)
rocket launch (16)
round (14)
ruler (7)

S
sad (4)
salad (4)
Saturday (15)
school (7)
school subject (16)
school uniform (9)
scooter (7)
September (13)
seven (5)
seventeen (5)
seventy (10)
she (3)
shirt (1)
shoes (8)
short (6)
shorts (1)
sick (11)
singer (6)
sister (2)
six (5)
sixteen (5)
sixty (10)
skiing (13)
skirt (8)
slow (7)
small (7)
snake (14)
sneakers (1)
snowy (13)
socks (1)
soda (4)
sorry (10)
South America (12)
Spain (12)
Spanish (12)
speak (12)
special (5)
square (14)
street (10)
student (2)
Sunday (15)
sunny (13)
sweater (8)
sweat shirt (1)
swimming (13)

T
tail (14)
tall (6)
taxi driver (11)
teacher (14)
teeth (14)
telling the truth (16)
ten (5)
tennis shirt (1)
Thank you. (5)
thanks (4)
that (7)
the (8)
theater (15)
their (6)
these (14)
they (5)
thin (6)
thirsty (4)
thirteen (5)
thirty (10)
this (2)
those (14)
three (5)
Thursday (15)
ticket (13)
tie (9)
tiger (14)
time (15)
times (10)
tired (4)
today (5)
too (also) (5)
too bad (13)
toucan (14)
tractor (7)
triangular (14)
T-shirt (1)
Tuesday (15)
TV (8)
twelve (5)
twenty (5)
twenty-eight (10)
twenty-five (10)
twenty-four (10)
twenty-nine (10)
twenty-one (10)
twenty-seven (10)
twenty-six (10)
twenty-three (10)
twenty-two (10)
two (5)

U
under (8)

V
very (11)

W
warm (13)
watching a movie (13)
we (4)
weather (13)
Wednesday (15)
well (3)
What about you? (16)
What color is it? (9)
What time is it? (15)
What's his/her name? (2)
What's the problem? (4)
What's the weather like? (13)
What's this? (7)
What's your address? (10)
What's your favorite subject? (16)
What's your name? (1)
Where's he/she from? (12)
Where's my cap? (8)
white (9)
Who's this man? (12)
window (2)
windy (13)
woman (12)
world (14)
wrong (10)

Y
yard (3)
yellow (9)
your (1)

Z
zebra (14)

NEW WORDS

Addison Wesley Longman Limited
Edinburgh Gate
Harlow
Essex CM20 2JE
England
and Associated Companies throughout the World.

© Addison Wesley Longman Limited 1998

ISBN 0 582 31885 8

Set in 11pt Souvenir

First published 1998

Printed in Italy by G. Canale & C. S.p.A.

Acknowledgements
We are grateful to the following for permission to reproduce these copyright photographs:
Ace Photo Agency for 19 right (Mugshots), 39 bottom left (Mauritius), 78 middle (Peter Hince), 79 top middle (Bill Bachman), 81 top right (Peter Hince) and 81 bottom right (Bill Bachman); Adams Picture Library for 79 middle left and 81 top left; Addison Wesley Longman for 37 top left; Addison Wesley Longman/Gareth Boden for 7, 21, 27, 29, 30 and 31; Addison Wesley Longman/Trevor Clifford for 111; All Sport/Tony Duffy for 42 left; Aquarius Library for 78 left and 81 mid centre; Ardea London Ltd for 106 top (Jean-Paul Ferrero) and 106 bottom (McDougal Tigertops); Australian Tourist Commission for 105 right; Bruce Coleman Collection for 97B, 97D (Christer Fredriksson), 104 bottom left (Alain Compost) and 105 left (Mary Plage); Camera Press/Tom Wargacki for 42 middle and 87 bottom right; Colorsport/Duomo for 86 top middle; Sue Cunningham/SCP for 105 middle; Greg Evans International for 39 bottom right, 79 middle right, 81 middle left, 81 bottom middle and 98; Chris Fairclough Colour Library for 79 top left, 79 middle centre and 81 middle top left; Ronald Grant Archive for 87 top middle and 89 left; Robert Harding Picture Library for 37 middle right; The Hutchison Library/J.G. Fuller for 97A; Image Bank for 19 left (Simon Wilkinson), 37 bottom left, 39 top left (Alvis Upitis) 39 top right (Elyse Lewin), 42 right (Alvis Upitis), 79 top right (Larry Gatz), 79 bottom middle (A Boccaccio), 81 middle right (A Boccaccio) and 107 top right (James Carmichael) and 107 bottom left (Margarette Mead); Kobal Collection for 13 top left (Stephane Fefer) 13 middle right (Richard Foreman); Frank Lane Picture Agency/Lee Rue for 104 middle and 107 bottom right; London Features International for 87 bottom left; Mirror Syndication International for 85 right; Philips Classics for 87 top right; The Photographers' Library for 79 bottom left and 81 bottom left; Redferns/Donna Santisi for 86 top left; Retna Pictures for 13 middle left (B Kuhmstedt) and 24 (Avena); Rex Features for 13 top right, 13 bottom left, 13 bottom right, 85 left (Dave Hogan), 86 top right (Pierre Suu), 86 bottom left (The Times) 86 bottom right (Juergen Hasenkopf), 87 top left, 89 middle (Pierre Suu), 89 right; David Simson for 10 middle; Tony Stone Images for 5 (Sylvain Grandadam), 10 left (Arthur Tilley), 10 right (Tony Latham), 37 top right (Don Smetzer), 37 bottom right, 68 (Pete Seaward), 78 right (Jon Riley), 79 bottom right (Andy Sacks), 81 top middle, 81 middle top middle, 81 middle top right, 97C (Adrian Arbib) and 107 top left (Tim Flach); Telegraph Colour Library for 37 middle left (A Tilley); Zoological Society of London for 104 top and and 104 bottom right.

Illustrated by:
Pete Beard, Kathy Baxendale, Celia Canning, Paul Cemmick, Debbie Clark, Phil Dobson, Clive Goodyear, Susan Hutchison, Tony Kenyon, Pat Murray, Chris Pavely, Liz Roberts, Graham Round, Jonathan Satchell, Francis Scappaticca, Jane Spencer, Andrew Thorpe, Lorraine White,

Designed by Jenny Fleet